uncovered feelings

uncovered *feelings*

OUT-LOUD WORDS ON
SEVENTY-ONE HAPPENINGS

Herbert F. Brokering

FORTRESS PRESS · PHILADELPHIA · PA.

contents

Copyright © 1969 by Fortress Press

Library of Congress Catalog Card Number 69–14625

A number of the sections of this book have appeared in altered form in *Greater Works*, official publication of The American Lutheran Church Men.

Designed by Otto Reinhardt

445J68   Printed in U.S.A.   1-7

The Apostles' Creed is old and I say it only on Sundays.
But it has a weekday feeling to me.
    It was good the way we said the creed today. Slow. Slow
enough to think and for everyone to say weekday words in between
the old sentences.
    The weekday makes the Sunday creed.
    We surely spoke up loud near the end:

1. *creed*

I BELIEVE IN THE FORGIVENESS OF SIN
for janitors who take dope and jump down your neck
for community leaders apprehended by the law
for people who spread rumors
for those who slam down phones
for people who transfer when they are mad
for those who read religious publications
for proud professors
for murderers
for bullies
for prostitutes
for priests and pastors
for my son.

I BELIEVE IN THE RESURRECTION OF THE BODY
for people I can't stand
for those who criticize my work
for ministers who don't like predecessors
for beauty queens
for my mother and father
for myself.

I am a believer, Lord, I do believe.

2. *pictures*

The five children were five years old.

They had not yet heard of the secular-sacred debate. Batman and God were painted in succession and hung side by side. They denied neither. They believed in both.

The cross was painted over the Lord as though he were crucified facing the cross. That was a new crucifixion painting. But not to the child. The picture carried the words *Jesus Facing the Cross.*

It hung alongside other titled works.

Noah Letting the Dove Out of the Ark.
A Rock Garden.
Our Bunny. (It was red, blue, green, and yellow.)
The Baby.
The Cat Lady on Batman.
Ready to Blast Off.
Baby in a Crib.
Ice Fishing.

Here's a Machine Making Lots of Balloons. (The green one popped.)
Now It's Summer.
He Lives in the Jungle.
A Color TV Set. (The set itself was painted red, yellow, and blue. The walls of the room, the wooden cabinet, and the picture were all in color.)
A Blackbird. (It felt as free and looked as easy as pouring ink on paper. Like a Rorsçhach inkblot of a bird.)
Airplanes Have Been Going All Over.
Beauty Parlors.
It's a Martian. (When you push a lever his hands go out.)

Ice Fishing and *Baby in a Crib* belong to the same boy. True.
Beauty Parlors and *Jesus Facing the Cross* belong to the same girl. True. They were five then. They'll be true when they are fifty.

3. *exception*

In the chronicles of the daily news China was now the enemy.
Ted was Chinese, but he was no enemy.
The news releases repeated the grim details of the yellow enemy.
Headlines from section A to section C resembled red and yellow
neon signs flashing alternately the words Chinese and enemy.
Every evening edition was like a ditto, ditto, ditto
to every morning edition.
Ted was Chinese, but he was no enemy.
Presses ran hard and struck bold black headlines in high letters.
A white student was struck to the ground, deep pain in his heart.
Minister! Minister! was the cry. A white man ran for a doctor.
Ted dropped to his Chinese knees for prayer. It was the prayer
of a righteous man, all news headlines notwithstanding.
Fast and furiously the petitions in Chinese filled the room
and the throne of God. The Chinese man was the great high priest.
The Holy of Holies was manned by a yellow man.
Ted is the exception to the rule, I thought as I lay there.
And there are always exceptions, which prevents man from ever
judging whole nations.

4. hanging

The young man could not be trained to kill an enemy. The young man was released and returned to civilian life.

The young man, who would not practice shooting an enemy, now hung on a tree. He hung by his tie. He did not belong to the armed forces, but he was baptized and belonged to the holy Christian church.

Of course the people were surprised. Amazed that a tie could do it. They were quite ready to help him down. It was easier than trying to help the boy up.

Few knew him more than by sight, before. They had not read his prose too carefully. They had not read between the lines. His loud poetry was in fine print and shuttled from editor to editor. His lines were camouflage and his readers never found him. He stayed hidden.

He hated violence. He found no peace in warring. He found no peace in the automatic tactics of the congregation. He multiplied the parables of Jesus by tens and twenties. He was not a boy to be easily bought. There were few bidders for the boy, and few buyers.

Both poetry and people had played tricks on him. He had many contacts and interviews, but choked on the accumulation of poem and prose lines, and promises that rhyme.

He had been let down.

Now they cut him down. They caught him confessing sin. The sin of the whole world. I cut him down.

I cut him down in the name of him who hung on the greenwood tree. I cut him down in your name, Lord. You know how a young man can end on a tree.

5. *tied*

The ushers had no bulletins.

The ushers had two pieces of rope per two people.

We sat two by two, tied to one another. Tied by foot and tied by hand. United, bound, joined by hand and foot.

Two by two by two by two we sat in every pew. As one stood the other stood. As one walked the other walked. As one knelt the other knelt.

We were conscious of every motion. There was always another in the same act. Nothing was singular or automatic.

I went to the communion table.
We both went. No one could go alone.
Together we confessed, ate, drank, walked,
knelt, stood, sang, and prayed.
   The pile of rope beside the ushers
was a sign of a very extraordinary hour
of communal living.
   Some debated the technique.
Some had nothing to say. For some there
was nothing left to say. It is doubtful
that anyone has forgotten the hour.
   The rope hangs over my desk. The man
to whom I was tied is on my mind.

6. globe

He held the globe in his hand. Plastic. Colorful. Well marked. He blew into it once more and it was a full-blown earth. The people watched the priest as though he were a magician.

Without a word he threw it out to the people. He yelled, *What will you do with the world?*

The surprised people batted it around until the plastic globe was in my hands. He looked at me and said with penetrating eye and voice, *Touch it. Pray for it. Hug it. Love it. Ask it a question. Sing it a song. Talk to it. Pass it on to someone. Who will it be?*

It did not happen quickly. He waited for me to do each thing he said. I sang it a song. I asked it a question. I spoke to it. But it was hard to give it to another. I did not wish to let go of the globe.

I did not surrender that globe. I shared it. We held it by twos. There were many present who wished that they might hold it a little while.

Lord, the gimmick globe is gone. Give me a hold on world affairs. A firm hold with both hands.

The child was five. He knew a clown when he saw one.
He knew a clown with his eyes closed. He knew what a clown is.

The painting bore the title *Clown Face*.

There was no hair, no chin, no cheeks. There was really
not a head at all, but it was indisputably a clown.
A big red mouth. Two big blue eyes. A bright balloon nose.
Four colored lines were a clown.

The child knew what truly makes something a clown.
That he drew. All else was unimportant detail.

So it was on every wall of the room.

Even as a clown is a mouth, two eyes, and a big nose,
so an elephant is a long nose with large flapping ears.

A flag is stars and stripes.

A bird is two circles with a beak.

A porcupine is a ball with toothpicks.

I could only wonder and laugh that five-year-olds
had discovered the design under layers of details.
So many designs, and each species of creation
after its own kind.

There are children who can draw me
with their eyes closed, Lord.

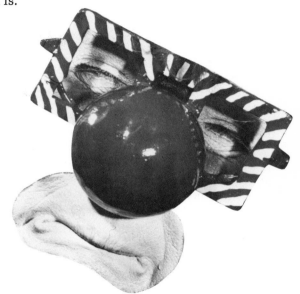

7. *clown*

It was Sunday morning. There were no ushers with carnations. I was 29,000 feet high, and there were four stewardesses in the aisle. What if a stewardess trained the church ushers next month?

8. stewardess

Good morning!
Welcome aboard.
You will find your seat in the front section.
May I hang up your coat?
Would you like a pillow, please?
You may adjust the temperature above you.
Please fasten the seat belt.
Observe the no-smoking sign.
Ask if there is anything we can do to make you more comfortable.
Would you like to look at Life, Time, Esquire?

In case of discomfort at high altitude, you will find oxygen in the compartment directly above you.
Would you like a beverage?
Will you have dinner later?
You will notice your choice of music channels on the headphones.
This is your captain speaking.
We are approaching our destination.
Fasten your seat belts securely for the landing.
I believe this is your coat and hat.
Come back to see us again.
Have a nice day.

Imagine the church aisle a busy service center, and all pews close enough for the ushers to reach and serve everyone on the Way. The hour or two is a fast trip. Barely time to serve each one, Lord.

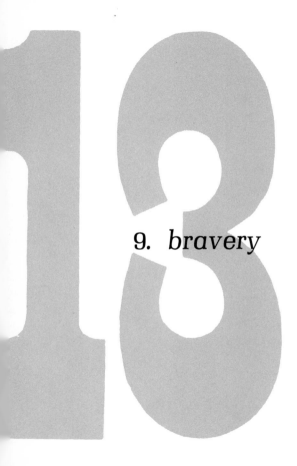

9. bravery

There had been a rash of crashes. Boarding the plane was a bit more than automatic, this time. Selecting cabin seats is always a guessing game. Where will the shade be? Where will the sun set? Who will sit in the next seat? Is it by a window? Where is the exit?

This time it was more: Where is the nearest exit?

And then, as if to defy it all, and act as though it really didn't matter and I couldn't care less, I chose seat #13A. No one had taken numbers 13A, B, C, D, E, F. It did something for my spirit to sport the only seat #13 tab aboard.

The fear was apparently nearly licked.

Through the gate came a famous professor. A theologian and seminary president. A man of high distinction, and greatly in demand. The world and the church could not think of losing this man.

It was a sign, that God was sparing us.

It occurred to me how much fear in me still was to be cast out. Between the presence of this man of God and defying seat #13, full confidence was restored to me.

That the professor sat in seat #18, and slept, made no difference. He was not really there to keep watch. His sleeping was a sign to me that God was keeping watch over the president, and me.

Later, I heard there was a little girl in seat #19. She did not know the president in front of her. What drove away her fear was that she had seen me, in seat #13, so obviously unafraid.

Lord, how we people depend upon each other for bravery.

His father was musical. He played in a combo and later in the city symphony. When we went to his house we'd always sing. He was the life of the scene and for fun we called him Mr. Beat. His feet were always going when there was any rhythm to be felt. That was years ago.

And that is his son, to my far right. Looks just like his dad. The hair line, the eyes, and the short chin. But he's not up there on the stage tonight. Not even in the last row. His father held the first chair for four years, and now he's directing.

Here's the boy, in the front row of the balcony.

It often happens. Rebellion, probably. Too much coaxing by the father. Probably pressure and lots of haranguing at home. Forced piano lessons, I'm sure. And when they finally got tired of arguing he no doubt dropped the whole thing.

You can tell he has some of Mr. Beat in him. All pent up. His feet are sure going. Just look! It must be a good case of father-rejection.

His feet are going like crazy.

But his hands. Let me see.

His hands! He hasn't any hands. Oh. You can tell, he was born that way.

He hasn't any hands and his feet are going like crazy. God, I spoke too soon.

10. mr. beat

11. yes

It was a baptism.

I told the deacons to sit down. There was nothing they could do.

I told the godparents to sit down. There was nothing for them to do.

I told the infant's grandfather to sit down. There was nothing he could do.

I told the father and mother and the grandfather and godparents to be quiet. There was nothing for them to say. Not now.

I went to get the child from them and bring him to the font. It was quiet in the cathedral. The organist was told beforehand there was nothing for her to play. Not now.

The Scriptures were read. The promises of God were read clearer than I usually read. Every thought was enunciated from the heart. I read the theme to the face of the child.

All were silent. By some miracle even the infant was still. The cathedral was more quiet than ever before. It was like a place for miracles in the middle of the night. In the midst of the long quiet, having read the promises of God, I half-whispered and half-shouted a threefold Yes. *Yes! Yes! Yes!*

God had said *Yes!* Unmistakably He had said Yes to the infant. Now it was the child's turn to answer God. For this he had all his life, to say a threefold *Yes, God! Yes, God! Yes, God!*

The threefold Yes still echoed in the corners of the chancel when I turned to the people and motioned for them to hurry forward. *Hurry! Hurry! Hurry!* I said. *Tell the child that God said Yes!*

My Lord, now that you have said Yes to the child there is so much for us present to do and to say to him.

12. cake

She was pouring the cake mix into the two pans. It was vanilla and the aroma and the scraping sound in the mixing bowl was like a signal. I knew the sound blindfolded.

I remember leaning over the bowl and wishing to be part of the batter as the spatula wiped it clean like a squeegee. The bowl was now much too empty and all that was left to say was, *Stop, Mom! Stop. Stop!*

It was a familiar cry in our house. Before she could do anything about the cry, Dad dipped the spatula into the pan and with one graceful swoop retrieved a generous helping and put it back into the mixing bowl. Dad was never far away at those cake-baking rituals.

There is no describing the feeling on the tongue and on the mind of a child at such a high and reverent moment. The feeling and the aroma were a promise of things to come and a pleasant reminder of a great event barely past. Cake batter left in the mixing bowl.

Small times like licking mixing bowls are momentous events in every generation.

Lord, crumbs and leftovers can be such a blessing.

13. *inside*

Somehow they wired the guitars and drums to light. The rhythm and the beat and the light and the sound are all one system. One piece.

The tempo of the drum and the tempo of the flickering blue are one piece. The quiver of the electric guitar and the quivering red lights are one piece. The tube waves of the electric organ and the tidal waves of green lights are one piece. It's all wired and soldered into one piece.

The people are dancing, inside.

We are inside the one piece of wiring. Inside the rhythm and the quiver and the tempo. Inside the red and blue and green. And, mostly, inside ourselves.

It is a loud, lonely place.

It is one room jammed with lonesomeness from wall to wall, floor to ceiling, person to person. There is enormous hiding space inside the volume of stereo stacked upon stereo, color climbing over color, beat bucking beat, and people passing people.

There are in this enormous one piece and one world ten thousand islands. It is a perfect atmosphere for imperfect aloneness. Insideness. Isolation. Lonesomeness.

Wiring does not do it.

The means is overcoming the end. The thing made is overpowering the ones who make it. I am in a metric, multi-colored monster. A fluorescent Frankenstein.

Lord, this is for me a confession of my sin, and a confession of my faith.

14. *out-loud words*

The Small Catechism was getting to be old hat. We had looked at the words of Martin Luther at least a thousand times it seemed. The question What in school is this book like? was no surprise. Nothing is much of a surprise after a thousand times of looking.

What in school is this book like? English? Social Studies? History? The surprise was not in the odd question. The surprise was in the unanimous answer.

Mathematics! The old book with the statements of faith was most like math to us.

In it the words stand for something else. They are symbols and signs. Words represent something beyond the words.

There was no doubt in our minds. The confessional writings of the church were most like math.

I believe that Jesus Christ,
true God,
begotten of the Father before all worlds,
and true man,
born of the Virgin Mary,
is my Lord . . .

was like numerals and numbers and symbols and signs. We decided to handle the words with care and accuracy and to check our answers out loud.

Confessional words are for out loud and for checking. They stand for something greater than themselves. The truth is what they really stand for. It's how they are finally used in living, O Lord.

15. *introit*

A thousand people were in the auditorium. It was a small town. Reformation service, televised. And if televised, then it should be something alive and moving for the viewers throughout the country.

The Introit for Reformation Day was the theme, and if a theme then it must be out loud. A thousand said it, in unison, in rhythm. A thousand of us said it with one voice: God is our refuge and strength; a very present help in trouble. God is our refuge and strength; a very present help in trouble.

It sounded like a chant. A marching song for soldiers.

Then we stood. We walked. A thousand of us walked in step with the Reformation chant. We walked the beat of the words:

> God is our refuge and strength;
> A very present help in trouble.

We felt the Introit. It had a sound. It had a rhythm with its words. It had a beat. It was more than words. It was our own words. It was a sentence with a meaning and it was as though we knew this meaning at once.

Since that day, the Introit is more than an ancient psalm to me. It is a theme song. It works its way from my head to my feet. It's what everything is all about. It is believing your words, Lord, from head to foot. It's knowing them, and walking according to them.

16. sermon

It was a sermon. Not the best but the only one for this day.

I could have slept, with some of the others. But I did not. I dared not. I never do.

I had to stay ready, waiting and ready for his sentence. Ready for the one sentence that was worth it all. I always come to hear all of it for the sake of the one sentence. All his preparing and all my listening is for the one sentence.

When he says it, I will hear it. There are thought gaps. Things he leaves out. Space. I fill in the gaps as he goes along. What he does not say to us I say to myself.

He does not try to say it all. He leaves blanks and spaces for me to fill in. I do.

He does not know when he says his big sentence. I know. It's when all the words become the one word. When all the thoughts become the one thought.

It's when the words become like flesh and blood to me. My flesh and blood, Lord.

17. *ready*

It was Communion Sunday. I didn't always remember when it came. Once I came ten minutes late.
When the bread and the wine were ready, he said, *Come, for everything is prepared.*

I was not prepared. I'd come ten minutes late. The confession of sin was just ending.
The special preparation was over.

I did not eat or drink with the communicants in my row. I did not go until the last table.
Then I hurried to eat and drink. Surely it did not depend upon ten minutes of special confession.
It did not depend on anything I might quickly do.

Here was a table always open to me. I was ready because of who I was and who He was to me. It was not whether I was on time; it was whether I was His.
I had been, since baptism. Preparation is more than a paragraph or prayer on page 251.

So I am continually ready for Communion.

That was not always clear to me, but it's quite clear now, Lord.

18. *snow*

Snow can make a city small. A snowstorm can make big New York City like a little town.

The sidewalks on Fifth Avenue are snow paths for single-file walking. People say Please and Thank you, and stand in ten inches of snow to let people pass them. The snow has turned the rush hour into a slow walk, and every man has this blizzard in common.

Moving autos are a curiosity. I have Broadway to myself. The news circling Times Square is my own. It shines through the snow like a beacon. The streets are at a standstill. The world goes on. The blizzard is not the only news.

Right now, gloves and galoshes are on sale. Hand-printed signs are sitting in the store windows.

Snow has slowed the city. A state of disaster has been declared. Strangers are brothers for forty-eight hours.

Lord, eliminate the disaster. Extend the brotherhood.

19. *ice*

The rain poured down. In sheets of ice. It was ten degrees above zero. Everything from grass to treetops was coated with ice, and high-voltage wires sagged like jump ropes. Oak and elm rustled like chandeliers in a breeze, birch bent like weeping willows and sprawled like a limp ballet chorus on a glassy stage.

The ice had come and in the dead of the winter all of us tree owners and tree lovers held our breath. I stood at all my windows and doorways afraid of the transparent load on every branch and pondering how I might bring relief to every tiny twig.

The radio blared. It was as though the entire agricultural department had rushed to the studio to warn all tree lovers. Do not touch! Do not tap off the ice! Do not spray hot water and melt the ice!

They were quite right. The burden of the storm was heavy but it was even. It was tolerable. Not even a mathematician could distribute so much weight more perfectly over so many square inches of trees and shrubs.

They were absolutely right. My poplar is tall again. The elm and oak are swaying. I am relaxed again.

Lord, I didn't panic. The scientists helped me keep my head, and my trees.

20. *font*

The cathedral in Ghent is famous for its paintings by Van Eyck. But that's not what I remember most about this Belgian house of worship.

There is a font for baptism in the west transept.

It is a giant globe. The shape of the earth. Taller than man. This font is not the shape of a basin or bowl; it is the shape of the world.

Coiled snugly around it is a serpent. It is a possessed world. The font is not a silver bowl; it is a fallen world.

Beside the font is a candlestick with the largest candle I have ever seen. It belongs to the complex of the baptismal setting. It is an enormous celebration!

On top of the possessed world is a gold cross. The fallen world is redeemable.

The baptismal globe is in halves. Above it a large pulley-and-chain anchor to hoist the font in half. Inside is water.

The font means everything baptism stands for.

In baptism God speaks. The child enters the world. He is placed into it for there he shall live. In this world he has a name and a mission. In his world is satan and a savior.

His world needs saving. In baptism he is sent into every corner to save it.

I went out wondering who among the baptized was saving me.

21. *gravestone*

A visit to a homestead in Europe is not
to be forgotten soon. The place where Father was
born and spent his boyhood, and from which he embarked
for the new world. To stand under his oak trees.
To find his letters to his brother, postmarked
North America, 1910, 1920, 1930, 1940. Small
sermons describing your own birth in detail,
and other joys or sorrows of the only son
in the new land.

Wearing wooden shoes in the pastures and
peat bogs mounts the excitement. But it is greater
still to stand on stone bearing the old family
name and an old verse from the Scriptures.

The gravestone was now two stepping-stones.
One before the kitchen; one before the barn.
The old gravestone, centuries old, split in half,
no longer bore the fifteenth-century date.
But therein lay the answer. Since 1463 my family
had lived on that land. It is hard to hold
together every heritage, souvenir, and sentiment
for five centuries.

So it happened once upon a time. The old
gravestone became two stepping-stones. One for
where they live; one for where they work.

22. *lintel*

The old adobe house had watched a century go by. Her light sandstone walls had housed people too numerous and illustrious to trace. In their days she was home, schoolhouse, meeting place, or church. She'd been a fortress.

Now her walls came tumbling down under the force of the bulldozer. Her days were done and she lay in a heap. The historical society and conversation club were too late. They were mourners.

In the pile of stone and fine dust lay rough lumber. Flooring, window frames, doors and their overhead lintels. That I could not leave. The lintel. The cedar log rough and scarred from old circular saw blades. The wood that held the doorway high for the innumerable illustrious of the past.

It is not possible to turn one's back on all that is refuse or junk. The cedar lintel now hangs in small crosses from coast to coast.

Only because fifty doors would replace the one could I bear the pain of the sandstone heap mixed with cedar. Where there had been one gathering there could be many. Where there had been one wall cross there could be fifty.

23. *confirmation tree*

It throws off the price of personal real estate to plant a confirmation tree in the front southwest corner of the lot. There it has been for more than a year now.

The hole was dug with more than usual excitement. The balled roots were lowered cautiously as though to surprise the soil. Water was poured in lavishly as though to quench a drought. The sod was replaced as though it had never been lifted.

Only the celebrating confirmand could tell the tree had not grown there from seed. It belonged to the property and the day. It was a green sign of a glad day.

It's hard to sell property with such a tree. How does one calculate the improvement? The property tax? The sales value? How does one move away from property that has a confirmation cedar in the front yard and a birthday apple tree in the back yard?

It is well to leave heritage behind. My tree took root. It will give others shade.

I invest in personal planting wherever I go. I am a mobile man. This will bind me to all the places I've ever lived in. I love the yard with the cedar in the southwest corner. Soon I may go away and plant a new tree. Perhaps it will be a wedding oak.

24. mokols

Mokols, they were called. No one else made them. No one else knew their name. A century ago a grandfather had brought the recipe to America. Mothers had passed it on to daughters and even sons. I was one son.

Now, four generations later, the family was in the land of mokols looking for mokols. Both name and recipe were lost in the land of the bearded man who brought the recipe so far. The tasty heritage could not be found under any frying-pan lids.

It was dinnertime in Austria. Being ten and being hungry sharpens the eye and the nose. Little will stop such a boy on his way to an empty table and a menu. He was ten steps into the old restaurant and he stopped dead like a pointer. *Mokols!* he shouted, pointing to the platter well tended by the hungry man.

There were Mokols. And they were as good as in the days when a man brought a new recipe and his bride to a new homestead in Colorado.

Every family has its secrets. Mokols is ours.

25. *ovation*

The convention was as so many are. The best.

Every speaker was applauded as though he were a celebrity. A keynoter. A star. To the two thousand youths all guests were celebrities and the air snapped with the clapping of hands.

Another man was next. His question was quick and clear: I've been hearing you greet your speakers. What would you do to greet Christ?

In a split second, applause broke out. It was like tidal waves breaking and thunder clapping at once. Four thousand hands would not stop the beat and the volume of the clapping. All stood like one man. It was an ovation. It was for the Lord.

They would not silence easily. It was hard for the man to hold up his hands to stop the applause. It was the longest alleluia, and the loudest, and for many perhaps their first real alleluia!

They did not stop until they had given Christ a very big hand.

It was not rehearsed. It was not approved by all. But it was done by all. There is probably none of the two thousand who has forgotten the night.

Praise, practiced in the pew, will break out anywhere.

26. *bedtime*

The father said it was bedtime.

But I can't stop writing the story now. I'm too afraid! The little girl had written her way deep into the dark. Now she must write her way out.

She did not look left or right but straight over the top of her pencil. The lead sped as swiftly as her feet in the woods. So fast did she run that proper spelling was quite out of the question. There was absolutely no time for punctuation and she wrote with ease words she'd never seen. Paragraphs were a thing of the past.

Her pencil stopped. It moved down to the next line. It was a new paragraph. She reached for the dictionary. She erased and corrected. I knew she was out of the woods. She took time for punctuation and caps.

I whisked her off to her bed.

She did not mind. She was ready to sleep.

She never minds the dark, unless it is inside her.

27. our father

It was his third time through the prayer. Every time his mind wandered off, so each time he started over.

His brain was on a kick tonight. Shapes. Earth shapes.

They swore the earth was flat.
They swore the earth was square and floated.
They discovered the earth was oblique.
I say the earth is a heptagon!

Perhaps this would help to get through the prayer. He'd stretch it around a seven-sided earth. This was no special problem, for he had toothpick models of hexagons and octagons and pentagons all over his room. If there really were seven prayers inside the whole Our Father then concentrating ought to be as easy as building a heptagon.

Before his prayer was done, he'd made seven careful trips around the globe. Thinking through a toothpick sculpture is a very careful operation. What a world!

It had a father.
It had a kingdom.
It had a will.
It had hunger and bread.
It had debtors and forgiveness.
It had temptation and strength.
It had evil and deliverance.

Now he was wide awake, for he'd thought of a new earth shape. A seven-layered world. In it there was no place without a father, a kingdom, a will, bread, forgiveness, strength, and deliverance.

In the morning he'd build a heptagon. He did. I know.

28. junk

There was junk everywhere.

Old tires, crates, a fender, galvanized pipes, half-chairs. Refuse. Junk of all sorts.

There was no junk like it in all the city. This litter surrounded the park like a metallic hedge welded, glued, nailed, and tied into one constellation. The park was like new. Quite new. And there was none like it in the world.

The asphalt was now green. They laughed as they anchored the sign, Keep Grass Green.

Those who looked, laughed. Those who labored from morning to evening laughed even louder. The whole project was a laugh. It was the first laughter the area had known for longer than anyone could recall.

It was a laugh. There was no junk like it. They painted it everything between white and black. What was litter yesterday was being landscaped today.

A clever reporter wrote, City Jungle Turns into Jungle Gym. A sermon theme read, Debris Redeemed To Be Dedicated. However they said it, old was now new.

They named the junk Joe. He was the man who crossed town and tracks to bring color back to a pale city. Joe said No, yet they called the old park Joe.

He's in another city now, with other junk. When they finish they'll name that junk Jesus. Jesus! That's where Joe got the idea to redeem the rejected.

29. *offering*

They had received the offering. It was not great for it was a small gathering. Nine, counting the guest. Each Thursday night it was their custom to invite someone from the street.

He was a man between thirty and fifty years. It was hard to tell for sure. His address was the city. His total property was the portable cot which he placed on whatever porch possible for fifty cents per night. It was his protection from the law and from lawlessness.

There was not much for the guest to offer. He put in two cents. It was all he had. He was embarrassed and he was bankrupt.

The plate had circled the group for they always sat around the table. They arose in behalf of all. She knew how, for it was their custom. She set the plate before him. *Take it,* she said. *Take it, for your eating and drinking.*

He smiled. Laughed, in fact. He was sure this was their ritual. He thought it was symbolic. It was real.

They convinced him, saying, *Offering is free. We give it to you.*

So he went out into the night with his cot and the offering. He was half chuckling or half sobbing. I could not tell which.

When the table was cleared two pennies were under his empty plate.

30. *hosea and gomer*

Hosea and Gomer in this age would be more the subject matter for domestic courts than for church classes. This prophet and his prostitute wife were the story of the week for the eighty-nine youths.

She left the prophet. He bought her back. Each time Gomer left Hosea he took her back home. At the auction it cost money. In his heart it cost mercy. He had enough of each.

It stirred their imagination. It was the plot for their Mercy Drama. It was the story line of a Forgiveness Ballad to follow.

There were many more lines than here recalled. Each had the redemptive refrain, *Here comes God with pay and mercy!*

Each stanza was split and the lines met each other across the large room.

I am love of God the Father.
I know God, but I can't bother.

No. No, no, no! Gomer's saying.
Yes. Yes, yes! Hosea's praying.

Oh the heart of me is yearning.
Let me go; the Baals are burning.

Gomer, Gomer, there you run.
Louder. Louder. Oh it's fun.

Stealing, swearing, lying, dying.
Waiting, praying, crying, sighing.

In the country; in the city.
Need for loving; need for pity.

Gomer. Gomer. Running. Hating.
Husband. Husband. You still waiting?

Come my bride, we need forgiving.
I was like dead, and now I'm living.

You grieve me, Love; my heart is sorrow.
I'll be back; at least tomorrow.

Here comes God with pay and mercy!

31. *incense*

The architect was a visitor. He was not known here. But he was known in every major city and sought by city planners. At home his studio wall was covered with citations.

His eyes were schooled for shapes of arcs and lines. His mind was trained for color, shades, and for the habits of the sun. His motto was to design with the earth. He had high regard for seasons and terrain. Builders had high respect for his sharp senses.

His taxi stopped by the church. It was a rather new church. That is where we met him.

It was evening. Prime time for stained glass. He asked to see the nave. Keys were fetched and switch boxes and panels were tried until every light was on.

How gladly we opened the huge doors. He stepped in. Not more than one long step. He stopped short. *It smells good, this has a marvelous-smelling wood.* That's what the architect said.

For seven years it had stood, and I in it every week. Its aroma had never come to me. Everyone kept saying how it looked. This man was struck by the smell of wood.

Come early, he said. *Before the people come with their perfume and sweat.*

I do. It is perpetual incense. The wood does not run dry of aroma.

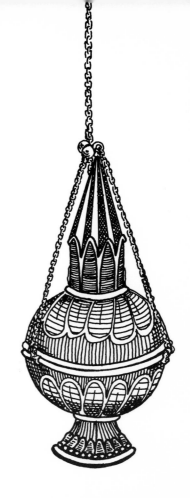

32. father

The children liked the questions. No one had ever asked them before. People like brand-new questions when the answers have lain dormant in heart and mind for years.

What is a father?

He makes money to buy toys . . . he buys animals for children to play with . . . he feeds his family . . . he makes a mother feel like he loves her . . . he is smart and intelligent and goes to bed late . . . he is a good cook, in an emergency . . . he is a man you can look up to . . . he is a man who punishes you when you do wrong, and helps you not to do it again . . . he is a man who keeps you from making some mistake by his own experience . . . he is a wonderful dishwasher, a clean-up man who gives to the handicapped and crippled . . . he is a man you can tell your troubles to . . . he wants you to go to heaven . . . he is a hard worker . . . he is a person who understands his children's problems.

How is a father like God?

He wants you to go to heaven . . . he guides you in the right way . . . he forgives . . . he doesn't let you get away with things . . . he acts like God . . . he wants you to be good . . . he works . . . he is the Lord's representative.

God works through my father . . . My father and God work together.

A good new question is like an open lock in a dam.

45

33. secret

    The house was full. The baby had not cried during the baptism and all the way home from church the mother praised the sleeping firstborn.

    As was the custom in this family, baptism Sunday turned into a kind of Christmas. Gifts surrounded the crib. A green shrub was potted and joined to the celebration.

    But neither food nor gifts could surpass the moment in this large family when the woman, now eighty-seven, brought her gift. It was neither wrapped nor visible. It was like a mystery to the tiny, magic to the children, and a miracle to the old.

?

As always, she approached the crib slowly. Slowly, and more slowly with each passing year, she stooped, and cupping her wrinkled hands she let them carry the secret from her lips to the tiny ear. She spoke only loud enough for the ear to hear. Her gift was always in the form of a whisper.

No one ever asked her what she said. That would be impolite.

From time to time, in some most unusual places, one could see her cupping her hands and whispering into all of our ears. It was the same whisper. So we always found out what the gift was. We did not discuss it. It was a secret. And we had all inherited it from the grand old lady.

Somewhere, in her early youth, she had read about the early church. In those days of long ago, the Lord's Prayer was whispered into the ear of the candidate for baptism. It was a gift for that great moment. She carried on the custom.

When a prayer is inherited in secret one learns to handle it with care.

34. *footwashing*

Men were gathered in a church. It was a convention, and men will do most unusual things away from home.

They talked about washing feet. One man did not remember anyone having ever washed his feet. No nurse, no mother, no older sister, no wife. He could only recall washing his own.

It did not take long. He and another man sat facing one another in the chancel. They were seated on small kneelers. The baptismal bowl and water was between them.

He hesitated to remove the shoe. The other man waited. Long. This was not a robbery. He must take off his own shoes. He did.

Now the socks. He hesitated again. Longer. Much longer. It was a natural question. *Why are you waiting?* Barely asked, it was answered. *Because I'm afraid my feet may smell.* When the laughter had died down every man felt the same fear for himself. The conversation went on, *But that's why I will wash your feet. To refresh them.* The socks came off. The footwashing was under way.

In a baptismal bowl.

A washed one was washing. A baptized one was baptizing. Water for the head was water for the feet. A loved one was loving. One ministered unto was now ministering. The meaning was no problem to the men.

The footwashing made a loud splash. Some men did most unusual things away from home. Now they are doing some most unusual things at home.

There was a passion for print.

What was said did not always count. They loved print. The layout, typeset, paper texture, and advertising could sell it. The printed page was out to make a buck.

Print can bridge distance. Print can also separate. Print can communicate; it can camouflage. Print can come close. Print can keep far away.

The phone rang. She spoke of the assignment I had finished for the class. Our conversation became hysterical.

No, I cannot send the brochure of the course.
But I can send a xerox
of the dummy
of the brochure
of the teacher's guide
for use with the study book,
for use with the student material
in the classroom.

35. *print*

That was the crux. I was to receive a carbon of the carbon of the carbon of the carbon of the carbon of the original.

Lord, keep what is printed close to the people and the present.

36. worship

The minister was on vacation.

The congregation held a happening.

They gathered in the parking lot . . . set off firecrackers . . . ate popcorn . . . sang a Thanksgiving hymn . . . folded their hands . . . said Amen seven times . . . walked in single file . . . took off their shoes in the vestibule . . . were blindfolded . . . heard the Scriptures read . . . applauded for five minutes . . . looked each other in the eye . . . took turns looking out the door through binoculars . . . turned on the rock 'n' roll station . . . read Psalm 23 with jazz on loud . . . read the Gospel out loud together . . . said three Yes's after each sentence . . . went swimming . . . touched breast and brow with the sign of the cross each time they entered the pool . . . bought the daily newspaper . . . rode the ferris wheel, shouting the headlines until the wheel stopped . . . fed each other ice cream . . . struck each other three times . . . screamed for help . . . shook hands . . . threw seed into a garden . . . chanted the Magnificat . . . skipped seven stones across the water . . . each time saying one of the seven last words of the cross . . . threw dice . . . chose up seven sides . . . had a relay race carrying a Bible on their heads . . . raced each other to the cars, praying the Lord's Prayer all the way . . . phoned each other upon arriving home . . . pronounced the Benediction upon each other.

Lord, I was in charge.

What shall I say to the minister when he returns?

37. brother

It was 1935. The college boy was home for Christmas.

The gun was clean and cocked. The air was brisk and it cracked under the rifle shot. The squirrel was hit and stuck in the high crotch of the limb. The hunter was a climber. The willow was frozen and brittle. The limb snapped. The branch broke. The boy fell. The boy was dead.

The boy was eighteen. His brother was nine. There were others who braved the weather for a Christmas burial.

It was now 1965. The little brother was back. He was there to preach. It was early on the hill in the country church. He was alone, waiting for the people, and remembering. An old woman was the first to come. She broke the silence of thirty years: *I saved the squirrel. It has been in the attic for thirty years. I will give it to you. You are older now.*

Her son had been with the college boy on the hunt.

The mounted squirrel was propped up by a dusty hymnal.

I have the squirrel. I wish I had the hymnal. In it is the song he sang as he left the house that day. We all remember the words. "A Mighty Fortress Is Our God."

The boy never got through college. So many still talk about him.

38. *orange cat*

The cat was orange and magnificent. It had more confidence stored in the sinews of its two pounds than the Saint Bernard had in his fifty pounds. As usual the dog went loping to his own back yard, with the orange cat tagging after him all the way.

I had other cats. But none like the orange cat. Why this mixture of magnificence, courage, and confidence?

Perhaps it was the color.

Orange. A loud color without camouflage in sight. A screaming color against the

black earth, the green grass, the white walk.
Orange. Not a quiet, blending color, but wild and free.

Orange has no hiding place. The only solution
for orange is courage. Confidence. To run when
others would walk. To be swift when the others sleep.

Orange was no handicap to my cat. It built
cat character. The camouflage is in the courage,
not in the color.

Color could be a handicap. But it gave my cat
solid confidence. It created in her a free spirit.

Lord, show me the powerful meaning of color.

The minutes of the convention were taken by the secretary. Everything that was moved and seconded and tabled and passed was on the books, as they say.

All the resolutions were on the books, closed inside the briefcase, locked into the typeset of printing blocks, cast into lead sheets, and preserved on 249 pages of dry ink. The minutes were bound in a blue cover and are selling for one dollar.

There must be another way. Who said they must end up inside a bound book?

I was asked to open the blue book and set loose the sections on stewardship, world missions, and education. I opened the pages and paragraphs and laid them on a page like a long poem. The composer took the poem, and the two-hundred-piece orchestra and choir performed it.

The minutes were now a Mass. The resolutions were carried by the tenors, the voting by the altos and bass. Cellos and trombones sent pages of print into the air. Books and files and annual conventions could not contain the words.

Some people were glad.

Some hurried out of the Minutes Mass to find their blue books. They double-checked.

Lord, some were glad, and some afraid.

39. minutes mass

They talked about having religion right to the tips of the toes. The ten were barefoot, under the shade of the oak. They set out to pursue the saying, Religion to the tips of the toes.

They thought. Chewed grass. Squinted into the sun. Snapped fallen twigs. No one spoke. This was thinking time.

Then talk came like a geyser. There was no room for all the words. New words. First words. Thoughts they had never thought before. Free speech.

Worship in the sole of the foot. Roll out the rug on the fifth Sunday. A thick, deep rug on every square inch of the church floor. No shoes and socks allowed on the fifth Sunday. Only bare feet.

The Sunday for feet. For digging toes into deep carpet. The silent Sunday. Soundproof. Soft walking for the procession.

It would be a Sunday for soft preludes and snuggling songs, she said. For Bible lessons about the feelings of man, he said. Like the healing of the lame one, the washing of feet, and wiping them and perfuming them.

And could we have a ballet anthem? I ask. They all agree! In bare feet. An anthem sung from the bottom of the feet.

Man has feelings, Lord. Uncover them.

40. *uncovered feelings*

41. *photographer*

I was walking the streets of the city with my good camera. My father was with me. I was fifteen.

There was a man ahead, on crutches. His legs hung like branches. He did not seem to miss them and he hurried through the intersection without apologizing or holding anyone up. His new legs were under his arms. He held them straight and they did what he wanted them to do. They were good, and permanent.

I had been taking pictures.

Shoot it! You don't see many of these, my father said.

Not so loud, Dad! I said. *How would you feel if you had crutches and this big lens of a stranger was staring right at you? No!*

I did not want it for my files. I did not need to go that far to replenish my stock. There was something here more important than photography.

There are times to shoot. This was not that time.

It's more than a hobby, Lord. And more than making money.

42. drums

He rewound the Tanberg recorder for the one-thousandth time and plugged it into two twenty-inch speakers. In the basement of a duplex it's enough to wake anything asleep in the house or block. It was midnight.

The volume was on loud!

There was no sign of anyone awake except the guests facing midnight in the basement. The preacher at the drums was more than awake.

The rock 'n' roll rhythm filled every square inch of tile, cement block, and open joints. The drum churned out a throbbing sound like a rehearsed tornado.

He turned the amplifier down to a whisper. He said three words: *The Lord's Prayer*. The amplifier went back to loud! The beat and tempo rose and whirled, and it was a new Lord's Prayer. All the petitions seemed more than present.

He lost track of time. Clock time. His beat was perfect. There was fever and healing in the air.

In the middle of the glad, gigantic patterns of rhythm his feet and hands stopped. He whirled to turn off the amplifier and with the same motion set the Tanberg recorder on rewind. He was done.

As the tape spun back and its counter moved toward zero, he said to me, without faltering, *Next to Jesus, the drums are the most.*

The way he played, I thought that quite a compliment, Lord. A big honor to Jesus.

43. celebration

With the telephoto lens on his new camera he sauntered through the city. This was a new camera-fiend with his first big assignment. Shoot for celebration! That was the only requirement. Shoot for celebration!

Candid celebration was the reason for the long lens.

Celebration in a city is a big assignment, whether for expert camera man, sociologist, city father, theologian, or teen-age photographer. Singling out joy in a bustling city takes more than good equipment.

From afar he stalked the celebrants, into department stores, to news-stands, bus stops, cabs, and before store windows. Only one smiled until noon and the boy was not fast enough to get the smile.

The darkroom confirmed the young photographer's apprehensions. Celebration is more than smiling. There must be other signs of joy in the city.

The company bought his celebrating photos and hung them under the theme Joy. In none was there smiling.

The boy is right, Lord. I was with him in the dark room. I know the city.

She sold the man an owl for the boy.

He had bought an owl for the boy, a hollow cast iron owl.

44. *owl*

What does it stand for? I asked.

The young man in Chinatown, wanting to please a tourist, answered, *You can use it as an ashtray.*

But that wasn't what I meant. Once more I tried: *What is it really?*

An incense burner, said the man.

But why the owl? What does the owl mean? I kept asking.

The young man ran out of Chinese history and turned to the old Chinese lady. She was of another generation.

Her eyes and lips met the owl with pleasure. She gave her answer as though reciting Scripture: *Everything has meaning. You know, the fish is slick and smooth.* Her hands wove a path in the air of a fish swimming: *Life is to be smooth.*

She held the owl: *Life is to be free. You never shut the owl in a box. Then he is no owl. Tell the boy, life is to be free. Like the owl.*

The cast iron was now far more than a trinket, ashtray, or incense burner. It was worth the high cost of $5.60, for it had a very high meaning for my son.

Signs of freedom are all around, Lord. All around.

45. clipper ship

The ship's hull was steel. Massive sheets of steel, afloat in the water for more than a century. The hull was heavy and thick with layers of pitch-black paint. The date of the old merchant ship was 1863. She was solidly anchored in dark oily waters. The night and the wind and the quiver of the hull gave every indication that the Star of India would once more set out upon the seven seas.

The era of the clipper ship was short and went quickly. She had raced the route from China to London in her prime and had carried crews now long returned to ashes and dust.

It was a quiet night. For more than one hundred years there had been a creaking and a rolling from stern to stem.

The empty mastheads leaned to and fro, and the ladders swayed far above like floating stairways. The ropes were taut and seemed to flex every fiber at the memory of fearless men climbing them in high winds. Sailing winds blew through the cross bows, wishing for the sails.

There was a remembering sound around the black hull of the clipper ship. She once carried daily bread to Singapore, and spices and slaves and vices and silk. Kings and slaves and wives awaited her docking.

I could not stay long. My jet flew out in forty minutes. A man can only stand so much time in a museum.

Lord, preserve my spirit in my heritage, and for the days ahead.

46. boring

But it's boring! she said. *The same thing we had last year and the year before that.*

Three times she'd heard it and already she was completely bored. Jesus' parable was boring, after three tellings. What then was the matter with the telling of them?

She was fourteen. In her life she had tasted over 4800 breakfasts. Yet there was no one more eager for breakfast. It was toast with sugar and cinnamon every morning for two years now. Orange juice, too, not because she wanted it but because it was healthy. She'd quit complaining. Over 700 times in a row. Boring? Cinnamon-and-sugar toast boring? Never!

But the story was boring. More boring than putting in hair curlers every single night. More boring than brushing teeth and making beds. More boring than seasons.

The toast and the sugar she could taste. The hair she could feel and see. Toothpaste she could taste and smell. Spring. she could pick and put into a vase. But a story. What could she do with a story she'd already heard twice?

If only a story could have a taste, an aroma, a feeling. If only it could be her own story and could be picked like flowers and tasted and worn.

I said, *What if the story were like something that actually happens to you?*

Then I'd want to hear it again! she said. It would be like a diary or an album or a personal letter.

Then she'd take it again as gladly as toast with sugar and cinnamon, Lord.

47. *to swear*

The boy was angry and he was hurt. Beaten on the inside. There were enough cuts and scars on the inside to kill a man. Being a boy saved his life and he shouted out of his hurt straight into the face of the chaplain.

I don't want anything to do with the church until the church learns to swear! That was what he said.

For all the years of his life swearing was the way he had found relief for his pain. Swearing was his language and without swearing the pain was intolerable. Swearing was like an aspirin and he indulged in it.

To his amazement, the priest agreed. He nodded. He listened. He had heard every bit of it. The anger of the boy was loud enough to fill the chancel and the nave and the balcony. It was loud enough to fill the woods and the swamp and the beds in Ward B.

The chaplain did not ask the boy to whisper. The bed was the altar. The boy was a kind of unscheduled preacher for the day. His whole life of nineteen years was on the top of his heart and at the tip of his tongue.

Amen! was what the chaplain said each time the boy spoke. Each time the pitch of his voice was raised, until he was as angry as the boy on the bed. He was with the boy, all the way. *God damn sin!* he shouted, as loud as the boy. All was quiet.

The church had sworn. Then, in peace the bruised soldier said, *Amen.*

I was in the next bed. I said Amen, too. How well I remember, Lord.

48. indians

Five old Indians sat around a drum. The open tent kept off the heat of the sun and was the only sign of a stage. The pounding of the taut skin echoed out across the highway, startling many a passerby. Tourist after tourist came to a quick stop, having followed the sound and sight of the drums.

The Chippewas were meeting to remember they were Indians.

The old and the young danced. There were few between.

The four-year-old boy danced through one hoop and then two hoops. An old man seated on the circle of logs coached and applauded from the side.

A women over eighty circled the drums with a dance she'd known all her life. She stepped spryly to the rhythmic whining and chanting of the five men. An old chief with twenty-four pounds of bells strapped on his ankles and a hatchet in his hand filled the hot summer air with the chill of sleigh bells and war sounds.

Birch-bark offering plates sat on a log. It was Sunday and for some of the travelers this was their church. They understood the story well. There was a kind of sermon to it. They gave generously.

I emptied the offering plate and set it out for the next congregation of tourists. For some it was a peace offering. They remembered the white raids of their forefathers. For others it was remembering their lot in the suburbs and gratitude that they would not go home tonight to the reservation down the road.

That was my child going through the hoops, Lord. I am training him to be an Indian in a suburb.

"This Is My Father's World." Hymn #487.

It was now being sung for the fifth time.

Once in a room' with six sides including floor and ceiling.

Once on a hill overlooking the lake and the moon and overhearing the splashing bass and the loon.

Once at an intersection of the city, with buses and cars and pedestrians taking the fast turns.

Once in the three walls and the fourth of bars in the county jail.

And now, the fifth time, in the restaurant, with the nickelodeon going full blast fifteen feet away.

A carload of us did it, just this once, to find the length and breadth of the Father's world. The final words of the five new texts are lost. Yet these I remember singing, in the five places of the Father's world:

In the rustling grass, I hear Him pass.
In the splashing bass, I hear Him pass.

49. hymn

In the rushing mass, I hear Him pass.
In the angry lass, I hear Him pass.
In the blaring brass, I hear Him pass.

The country hymn had gone to town.

It had literally gone to town, for that too is your world, Lord.

50. *robot communion*

Someday a robot will serve the Supper. We'll be able to step up to a vending machine, put in a coin offering, and receive the bread and wine. A recording will repeat the Words of Institution and the Lord's Prayer while you stand there eating and drinking. That's what the man said, and he was serious.

The people were astonished. There were forty, between the ages of twenty and thirty, but they were staggered by the idea. It was enough to make them all say what they thought.

Vending machines can serve a multitude in a minute, but . . .

Vending machines can be kept sterile and healthy, but . . .

Vending machines can repeat Bible verses and prayers (well enunciated by professional readers) and they can be designed to look personal and more intimate than one hand in a hurry to get all fed within the hour, but . . .

There were reasons galore, yet they were unanimously against the robot. Main reason: too impersonal!

I made the motion we examine our own Communion practice. It was seconded and discussed. We voted unanimously to do away with all impersonal elements that have invaded the worship forms of our congregation. I am chairman of the subcommittee appointed to redesign Holy Communion, to get rid of all robot tendencies.

We are presently thinking of moving the altar and the pews, Lord.

51. *alleluia yippie!*

He said Alleluia! Three times.

Then they all said it. *Alleluia! Alleluia! Alleluia!*

It had no special sound as I heard them. Only three Alleluias by twenty-seven youths. Not one knew the meaning of this ancient word.

An engineering student suggested Yippie! We said it three times. *Yippie! Yippie! Yippie!* It was louder than the Alleluias and sounded more like seventy-seven than twenty-seven.

Then we applauded. The rehearsal was over.

I divided the group. Three choirs. Nine and nine and nine. Nine saying *Alleluia!* Nine hollering *Yippie!* Nine applauding! Simultaneously they performed, some against their will. It was a magnificent mixture of the old and the new, the classical and the vulgar.

That evening we went back to the threefold Alleluia. It did not sound like twenty-seven. It was more like seventy-seven. Without a word of explanation everyone knew the mood and meaning and volume for *Alleluia!*

We sang the exclamatory with an exclamation mark, Lord!

52. wedding

They did not want a wedding inside the church.

So it was an outside-the-church wedding, between the cabin and the lake. The groom was a writer, and he built a birch altar next to his homemade writing table. It all took place at the edge of the water.

The man had set the altar as his table. The cross, a large clay pitcher of water, and a long loaf of fresh Italian bread.

They stood before the altar and the guests scattered in the woods heard them declared man and wife. There had been no rehearsal. Everything was a surprise. Now there was another surprise. A new act for a new husband and wife.

I turned to the altar, took the bread, and laid it in the hands of the man. He received the bread without hesitating. This was not a rehearsal. This was no gimmick. He had brought this bread for his wife. He understood the meaning.

He broke the bread and gave it to his wife. She received. She broke a piece and gave it to him. They kissed, smiling, glad to be caught in public in a new act. With crumbs on their mouths they smiled with all the people, for all had caught the meaning.

They tell me he still breaks bread for her and she for him. And they drink out of the same cup. In your name they do this, Lord.

53. *wall*

There must be a better way than scratching JIM + JILL on the ceiling of the cabin. I counted. That made 417 initials scrawled in the rafters, walls, ceilings, and doors of Cabin #5. Lipstick, spray paint, ink, pencil, magic markers, shoe polish, and knife, all had made their debut there. They all sneaked by the huge sign, PLEASE DO NOT WRITE ON THE WALLS.

There must be a better way, it seemed. Like an autograph wall. One wall dedicated to the names, years, months, and loves of all the cabin dwellers. A diary and abbreviated biographical sketchbook without lock and key.

I framed the south wall and painted the frame red and blue.

Now there is a panic line for Cabin #5. Letters arrive long before registration time: Please try to put me in Cabin #5.

The wall is full. There's no room for writing. The carpenters are coming today to hang a new wall, with panels and hinges. The south wall will be ready tonight for a second layer of names and lovers.

I can take down the sign PLEASE DO NOT WRITE ON THE WALLS.

They have found a place to place their names in public, Lord.

54. *ouch!*

Large rusted spikes were wedged into the post salvaged from the fence pile behind the deserted barn. It had no use beyond firewood. Except that this was Good Friday and children were gathered for worship.

I set the post before them. It leaned into the chancel and tiny pieces of bark gathered on the rug. None were surprised or offended. The children were small.

I was more like a magician than a minister. They expected something like a surprise. It was the question: *How is this like Good Friday?*

The hands flew up and the answers tumbled in like a spelling list:

> *nails*
> *suffering*
> *pain*
> *wood*
> *dead*
> *old*

They were willing to go further. I did: *Tell me in one word what Good Friday is.* The list was shorter:

> *dying*
> *suffering*
> *killing*
> *hurting*

Then came the answer all understood:
> *OUCH!*

Good Friday is Ouch! All agreed. Without an official balloting it was obvious. There was not a dissenting vote. When Ouch! was said, no words followed. Everything had been said on the subject of Good Friday.

What then is Easter? A tiny voice volunteered the final answer:
> *ALL WELL!*

Easter is All Well! Lord, after Ouch!

55. *blue monday*

It was Monday morning. Blue Monday for the men and women who rise early to keep their appointments with the judge in criminal court.

These pews were no church pews. They sat as hard, looked the same. The mercy seat was in front. A kind of judgment place with a judge in a black robe.

Thirty-four men sat on the side, lined up like a men's chorus ready for the anthem. They had not rehearsed an anthem and they did not wish to sing.

Names are important at a time like this. One by one their names were announced. With it the brief charges against them, the reason for the appointments.

I remembered the childhood song Ten Little Indian Boys. Only now there were 27, 28, 29 Indians. Twenty-nine Indians out of thirty-four men. The charge in every case: Drunk!

How could that be? Eighty-five per cent Indians. Twenty-nine Indian men in this tiny courtroom at nine o'clock Monday morning. I did not know there were twenty-nine Indians in this city of a half a million.

At least it was not Blue Monday for the judge. He bent his eyes down to each man and he saw them. And to those who said *Thank you* he said without fail, *You're welcome.* And he meant it.

Today it seems there are many more Indians on the streets of my city. Many more than twenty-nine. Apparently they've always been here. I had to go to criminal court to discover the American Indian, Lord.

56. *for god and man*

She was known to smile a lot, at God and man.

Now it was night on the ground, deep in the woods. It was as black as the bear now gnawing on her shoulder, and deaf to screaming.

Not many nights before, in the city, he and she had scanned the sky for meaning. The stars helped them to talk. The sky was the conversation piece. It hung there suspended like a diamond mine they had just uncovered. The talk turned to the Maker of the mine. God and man were very much upon her mind. God and the woman were in his.

She screamed for God and man, but the bear would not drop her. Inside the deep woods, and inside the sleeping bag zipped tight over her head, there were no stars. Darkness covered her world as she tossed and cried and writhed in the arms of the beast. The grizzly was ripping for flesh and his heavy breath and brute power were horrible and frightfully new to the girl.

Four hundred yards from the resting place they found her. Beaten and in shock. She had lost too much blood to the bear, but they could still hear her plea for God and for man.

I was the man. A priest. For thirty minutes I was for her God and man. That is all the time she had or needed, to quit crying and smile a lot.

I left her smiling, Lord.

57. *fellowship*

Eeeeek!

At midnight, eeeek in a cabin could only mean an intruder or a spider or a cricket.

It was an intruder and his four friends.

Five mice can look like an army to a little girl in the top bunk.

Eeeeek! Don't hurt them! No! Don't! all became one sentence. Killing them was not the solution. Of course not. Nor was this the remotest possibility for visitors who seemed to come and go by some magic.

A flashlight was neither protection nor weapon.

There was but one solution. Receive the mice for the night. Prepare a banquet for them. A feast of pretzels in the corner.

The night passed quickly in sleep for the girl. The night was long for the five visitors who feasted quietly at the prepared table.

It was a good night. It was a good morning.

Very good, for there had been no murder in the cabin that night, of mice or girl.

The next night the menu changed. And it was most appreciated, for the table was spotless in the morning.

Fright had turned into fellowship, Lord.

58. *workbook*

Two hundred third-graders were waiting to see the large black and white photo. She held it high. It was very large, and they could see that an early frost had caught the pumpkin off guard. The leaf and stem lay limp. There was no rejoicing in the pumpkin patch.

They could hear the sound of the pumpkin leaves.

Ohhh.
Booo hooo.
Waaa.

They knew the color.
Color it black!
Color it blue!
Color it purple!
Gray!

She went on. *Who will do what the picture is doing?*

There were two hundred volunteers. All at once they became one enormous choir of motion. They bent and hung and drooped their heads and arms and hands and torsos and tongues like limp pumpkin leaves, and they made signs of weeping and crying.

The photo was replaced. They were more than ready for the next. It was spring, and new ferns fanned the sky to prove it. In no time at all the same two hundred children were on tiptoe, grabbing the air with two thousand fingers and screaming and shouting every sound of joy they knew. The fern photo was loud to them, and they were loud.

As quickly as they had gathered, they returned to their desks. The world is their workbook, Lord. Every page is real.

The professor phoned: *I want to go and I want to take the family. But I don't want to take our horse. All the children insist that the horse go too.*

It was critical enough to run up the long-distance phone bill. What about the horse?

I asked if the horse was broad and flat on top.

59. *altar*   *Yes,* he said. *Like a table.*

He had said it first. *Make it your table. Your altar table,* I blurted. It came as something of a surprise to both of us. *And put your green clerical stole over the horse. And get a candle and a cross and set it beside the stole. On the horse, of course.*

The professor did not hang up quickly. He understood that in some peculiar way the horse was to be the family altar for a while. It was to be the place for the eight to gather and decide the welfare of each other.

He told me later that the horse went. All had a very good time. A most excellent time. So did the horse, who was for a while an altar in the professor's household.

There is hardly a place, it seems, where stoles cannot be hung or candles set. There is no place that cannot be hallowed, Lord.

60. *home*

They took the Indians to the Guthrie. For one evening in their lifetime the five Indian braves were in the midst of the dazzle and glitter and buzz of the theater. They sank into the red upholstered seats and could have touched the stage with the tips of their long arrows. They drank cold soda from pink paper cups during the intermission. They smelled perfume and looked twice at ermine and silk which their squaws could neither buy nor steal.

Performance time was 8:30. They had come early, to be exposed to the culture of the white man's theater. They stared into mirrored panels. They threw new pennies into a gently flickering fountain and were encouraged by their guide to make wishes. The braves rubbed shoulders with critics loitering solemnly in the halls, and looked without comment at huge oil paintings, each marked clearly with names and prices on small white cards. There was no Indian name among them.

The last curtain call had been squeezed out of the smiling performers. The big squeeze was on in the corridors and the parking lot.

There was no charge for the big evening. It was part of an experiment. All their host required was a taped interview of their reactions for his committee Monday night.

The five braves were glad to see their reservation up the road. They had never especially liked soda or white shirts.

For all five their wish had come true. It was good to be in the reservation. Lord, there's no place like home.

61. *genesis 1*

On a trip you worship where you happen to be. It was 9:15 a.m. Sunday. A handful of people had filled the small church to capacity.

The guest preacher was not from Yale or Oxford. But he had come directly from the Indian reservation outside the city. What graduate courses had not taught him in public speaking he learned from his guitar. What he had never read in a library he had seen in the sky and uncovered in the woods of the reservation.

Genesis 1 is only one chapter. But it grew in length that hour. He sang a refrain that swelled the Creation story into a full-fledged song. All vices, ancient and modern, were listed in ballad form. Each received the refrain, *God made man too big for that!*

The power of the Creation doubled in the hour. In his chording after every refrain there was time for the spirit to soar.

The sermon did not have three parts. It had ten or twenty parts, as I remember.

The last stanza, which was no doubt the event that must have shaped this young preacher's text, went something like this:

> *God made the eagle to fly.*
> *Do not lock the eagle in a cage.*
> *God made him too big for that.*
> *God made the eagle to fly.*

He wasn't from Yale or Oxford. He will never appear in print. I cannot forget him. He quadrupled the meaning of Genesis, Lord.

62. road

It was a long road. Four hundred meters. One quarter mile.

It was a hard road. Hand-chopped rubble from the bomb piles of Berlin. Youths from foreign lands carried each whole and broken brick and pressed or crushed it into the new road.

It was a good road. Once their countries had been at war. Today they were sharing their war tunes, rehearsing them, memorizing them. With the rubble remnants of war in their hands they recalled what needs to be remembered in order to be forgotten.

It was a glad road. It could have been finished sooner, had they not laughed and talked so much. Had they not held hands and fallen in love here and there. The war was done. Hate was done. The road was done and the glad day of dedication was at hand.

It was a dedicated road. A cornerstone waited in the curb. The thirty young builders bent to lay their names in a bottle that went into the ground. Names and daily drink was what the construction project was all about. A tattered work glove, every finger worn through by the sharp edges of rubble, covered the milk bottle like a fine linen cloth. The cornerstone was shut and sealed with fresh cement and a song.

The cornerstone would not stand the weight and weather of a decade, but the thirty were ready to withstand storms more severe than weather. The ceremony was but a sign of the amount of dedication transpiring deep inside thirty minds.

Somebody has to haul the rubble, Lord.

63. amen

There were no tenors in the choir. The anthem would have to wait. I gave them words without music. I called it *Amen.*

The directions were simple. *When I say Amen in this next hour, you say what it means.*

They were lost. I gave them the script. Fifteen times there was an Amen; and each time, the choir broke forth with a new meaning.

Amen. *That's right!*
Amen. *You said it!*
Amen. *It's true!*
Amen. *Count on it!*
Amen. *Sure!*
Amen. *It can be done!*
Amen. *It's a promise!*
Amen. *Let's go!*
Amen. *Okay, Lord!*
Amen. *I'm counting on it!*
Amen. *Make it so, Lord. Make it so!*
Amen. *So be it!*
Amen. *Yes!*
Amen. *Yeah! Yeah!*

Amen is not a finale. Amen is a beginning. It's the sure spirit that sets out to *do* the prayer. It has a very eager spirit.

We did not miss the tenors that day. We did not miss the anthem.

We had our hands, and hearts, quite full, with a new piece called *Amen.*

64. *backwards*

The people no longer heard the prayer. They'd said it so many times. He said it backwards and they wondered where he'd learned it. And they learned to say it forwards again.

Father, yours is the glory.
Father, yours is the power.
Father, yours is the kingdom.
Father, deliver us from evil;
       lead us not into temptation;
       forgive us our debts, as we forgive
         our debtors;
       give us this day our daily bread.
Father, your will be done on earth, as it is in heaven;
       your kingdom come;
       hallowed be your name.
In heaven.
Our Father.
Amen.
I said it backwards once, and gave the prayer back to them.

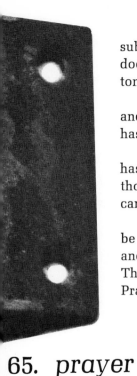

Each boy and girl had a photo in hand. The subject was prayer. They stared at the photos of doors and pods and winter scenes until their tongues were loosed:

Prayer is a door. It has hinges. It swings open and shut. Man goes in and out in prayer. Prayer has motion. People who pray really move.

Prayer is a broken pod. A burst of seed. It has many tiny parts. Everything said is like a thousand more things. It doesn't hold itself in. It can't. In prayer a man really lets go!

Prayer is winter. It's a waiting period. It can be a long or short season. It has lots of patience and silence. It hopes. Spring comes after winter. The seed and sun will break through the ground. Prayer is holding on with hope.

Prayer is a pumpkin on a vine.

Prayer is a rope with a tight knot on the end.

Prayer is seed on the loose.

65. *prayer*

Prayer is a window.

Prayer is a door half open.

Prayer is a bud at six in the morning.

I was not surprised to hear them say these things. They were surprised, Lord.

89

The nurses came to worship with stethoscopes, thermometers, heating pads, and syringes. Two came with teddy bears. Well-worn teddy bears.

The night before, they had agreed to bring a new kind of offering. Not envelopes. No money. But a bit of their life. A bit of their work. A bit of their play. A bit of their heritage. A bit of their daily bread.

The fifty nurses covered the altar with syringes and medication and love letters and teddy bears and note files and one rag doll.

Each stood up to tell why she had brought this offering.

Each offered it as a piece of her personal life. It all lay open before their fellow nurses, and the Lord. It was not like sealed envelopes and secret pledges.

There was a consecration of the syringes and all syringes, the stethoscopes and all stethoscopes, the rag doll and all rag dolls. It was the consecration of their lives.

They returned to their dormitory and took their offering with them. None of it had been on an altar before.

Now all their work and life was on an altar, Lord.

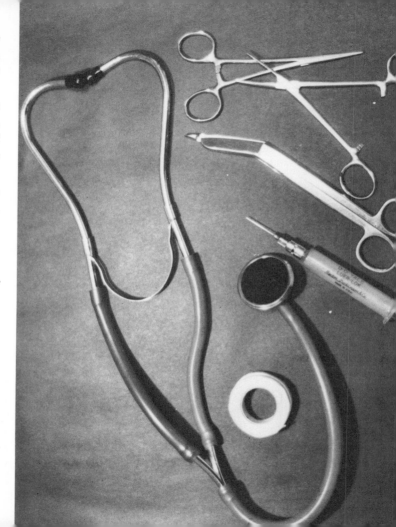

67. green

It was an art exhibit at kindergarten. The walls were covered with watercolored pads and hung heavy like a gaudy circus tent. Clay molds of turtles and birds and baskets of eggs and snowmen clung together with their last bit of energy. The teacher held her breath as once more and hopefully for the last time she reconnected them with toothpicks and glue.

The parents were coming!

Among the rows of paintings was one that deserved to be auctioned on the spot for a high price. It bore the happy title *Summer*.

Winter had been very long for the boy. The grass was barely green now, but it was coming. So the picture carried everything a summer could be.

The boy had summer pegged. He had put it on the paper without hesitating. It was one great concept.

In the painting the grass was green. Long and green. In the painting the face of the child was green. Bright green. And what would summer be without a brilliant sun? The masterpiece had a sun, painted brilliant green!

In this bit of paint the boy had said what all the people were saying. Summer is green!

The little boy told me once and for all what all the brilliant teachers had not told me in all my life. So much of the world is green. Absolutely green, Lord.

68. *wild and free*

The terrible lightning was gone. So was the mother racoon. The ground was soaked and her wet babies shivered behind the shed boards, orphaned at night. Six baby racoons were found and up for adoption.

What are two racoons added to hamsters, guinea pigs, rabbits, snakes, turtles, lizards, white rats, cats, dogs, and salamanders in suburbia? One is hardly overwhelmed by two more racoons in the north window well.

The book said to feed them, love them, and give them freedom. That meant, no collar, no leash, and no wire pen. Only food and love and freedom.

They come and go.

Early in the morning it occurred to me. They are neither tame nor wild. Can they ever go back to the wild world? They are weened now. Must they not become wild?

Somehow the two racoons must go into the woods and learn to fight for their freedom. The north window well will not teach them what their world calls freedom. They must gather food with their long claws or they will one day go hungry. They must seek freedom and fun with their snarls and barks, or their great trust of man will surely become their trap.

They seldom come back. They are almost wild, and free.

To be wild is their life, Lord.

69. *clarity*

The man was cocky. He and the boys were to have a last fling tomorrow, and then the wedding. It was to celebrate and commemorate all the freedom he'd had and would now lose. The fellows had some very elaborate plans.

But first it was now. The rehearsal.

With this minister it took longer than most. He insisted that everyone know the meaning of everything. He always took longer and that's what was happening now. He was on the words *The husband is the head of the wife.*

The fellows were all there and they rubbed their hands and looked at her. So did the .groom, the head of the wife. The men were grinning.

The minister must have seen this. He seemed to miss nothing. He had eyes and ears all over. He hesitated long enough for the chuckles to stop. It was quieter than before. He mentioned the man's name, including his middle name. He said it very distinctly, and went on: *You are to be the head of her just the way Jesus Christ is the head of the church—He gave himself for her!*

Turn to the front, he said. I did. And facing the crucifix he had me repeat after him the words about being the head of the wife.

It clarified two things: me and the wife, and me and you, Lord.

70. happening

The teacher was gone. We were teacher today. We had a Christmas happening.

The sign on the door said: You have nothing to say . . . we came in and sat silently . . . in a circle . . . we were blindfolded . . . each made a wish . . . the leader said, *In the name of the Father and of the Son and of the Holy Spirit* . . . we smelled perfume . . . tied the blindfolds into knots and threw them into a box covered with X's . . . shouted *The Lord be with you!* . . . scanned a newspaper . . . winked at someone three times . . . pretended to run . . . heard the leader shout, *Stop in the name of the Lord* . . . found a partner . . . stared at someone while saying the Apostles' Creed . . . put water on each other's foreheads . . . whispered the Lord's Prayer into someone's ear . . . passed *God is love* like post office around the circle . . . turned our chairs back to back . . . sang I Love to Tell the Story . . . off key . . . blew up a balloon until it popped . . . applauded . . . knelt in a circle . . . passed around a loaf of bread, each eating a piece . . . sang Silent Night while shooting cap guns . . . plugged one ear . . . heard Luke 2 read by the leader . . . applauded . . . sang Joy to the World . . . applauded . . . left quietly . . . with all the classes staring at us.

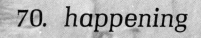